IF YOU CAN DRAW THESE THINGS → △ ∧ S ⌣
YOU WILL BE ABLE TO DRAW □ ⊓ . | WWWW
ALL THE THINGS IN THIS BOOK. O C D

FOR INSTANCE —

THE BOTTOM ROW TELLS WHAT TO DRAW

THE TOP ROW TELLS WHERE TO PUT IT.

VAMPIRE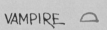

V V   V V

▲▲

■

▍▍

▼▼▼ ▼▼▼▼

VAMPIRE

GOBLIN

CAT

MONSTER

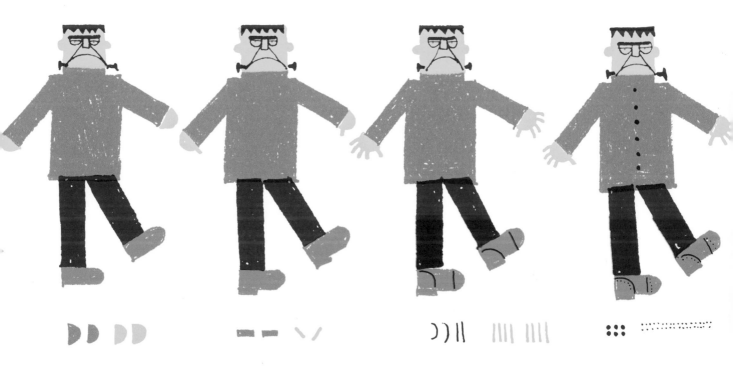

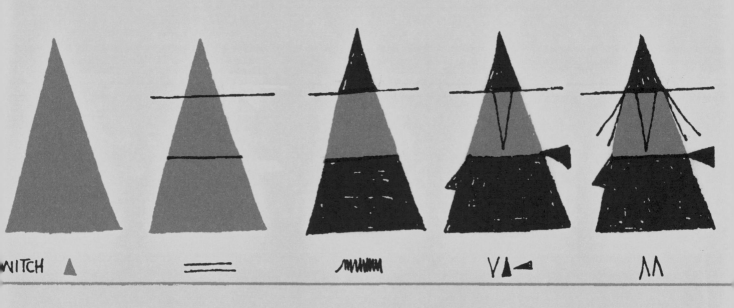

WITCH

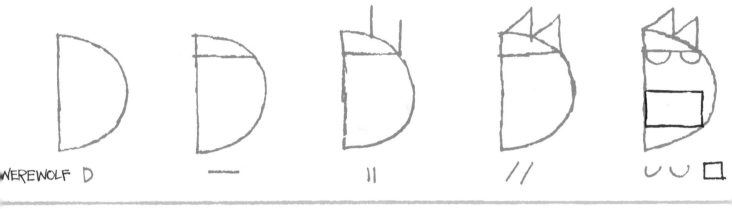

WEREWOLF

DEVIL

13

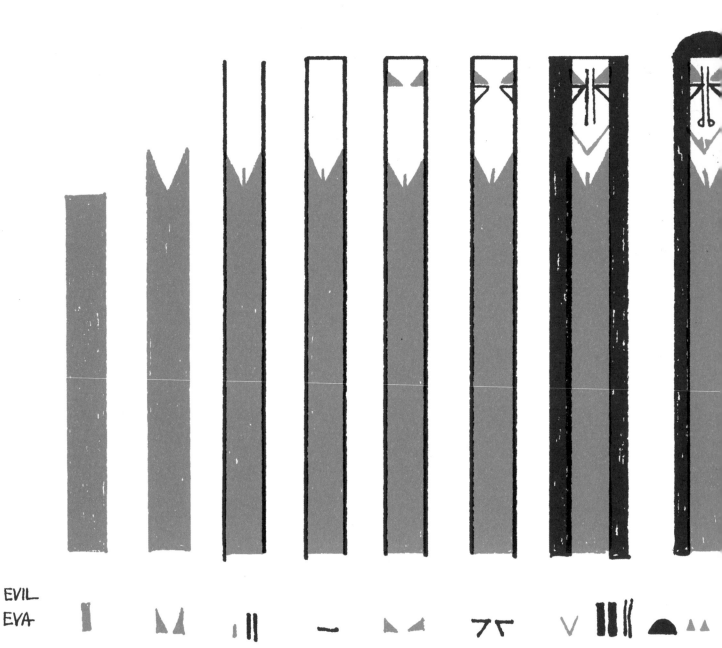

EVIL
EVA

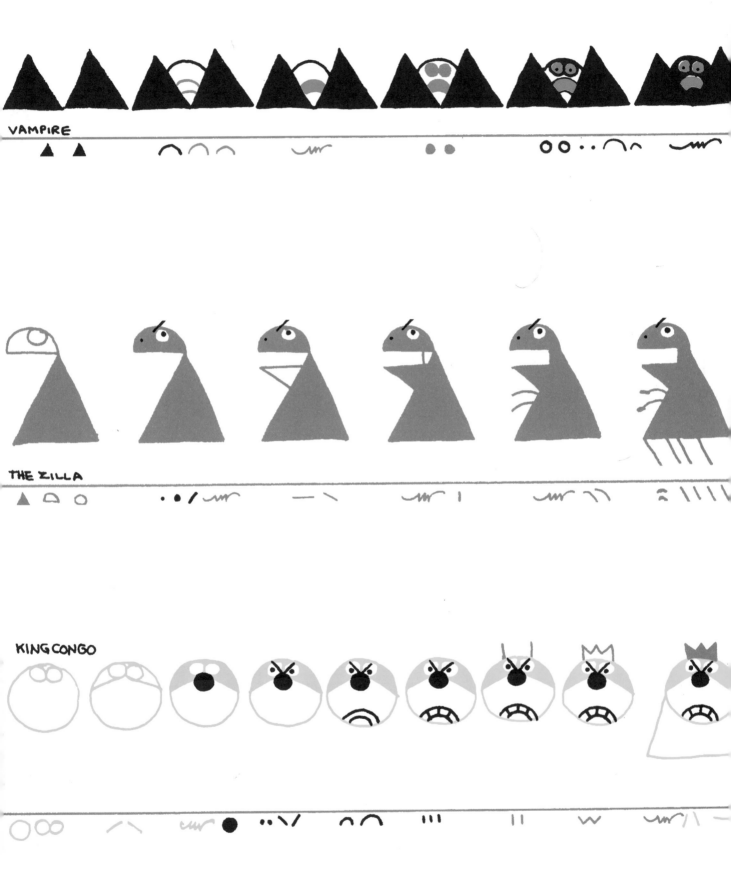

VAMPIRE

THE ZILLA

KING CONGO

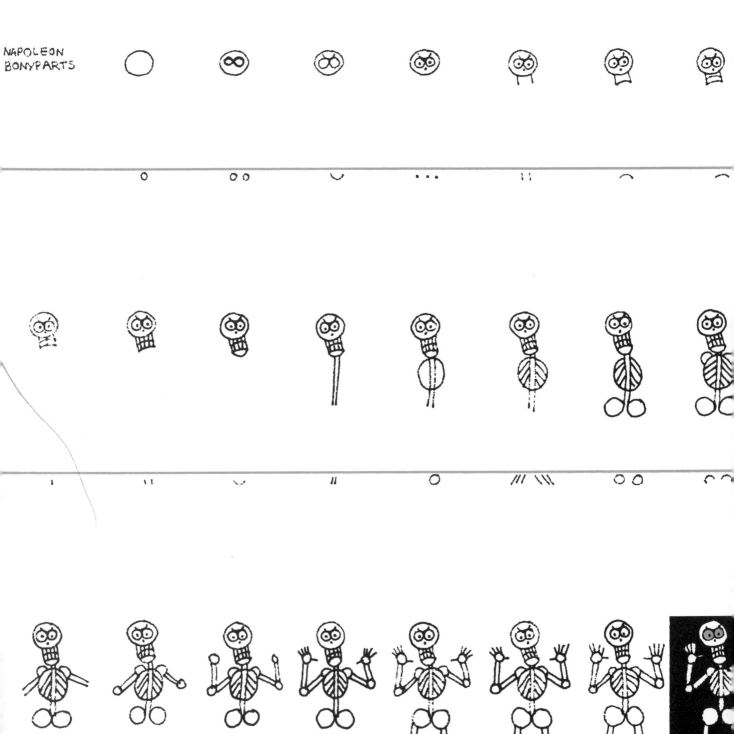

ALSO

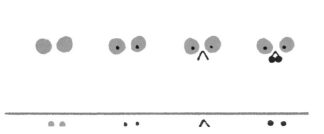

NAPOLEON BONYPARTS

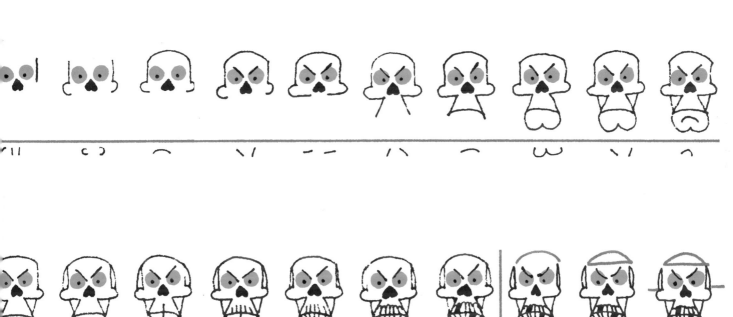

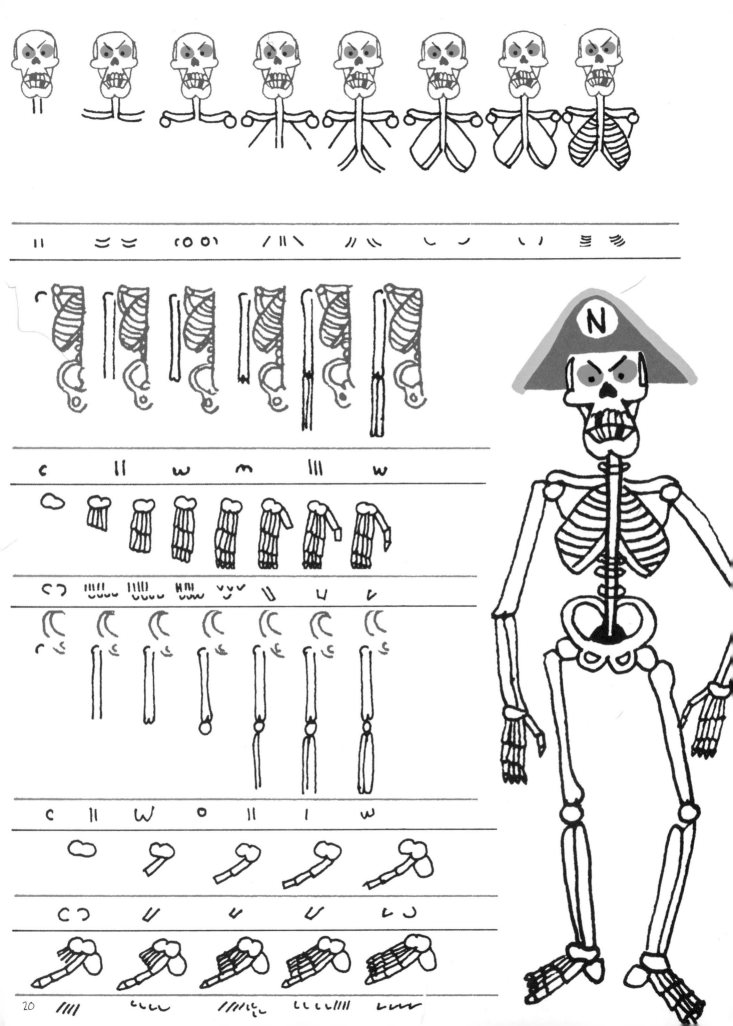

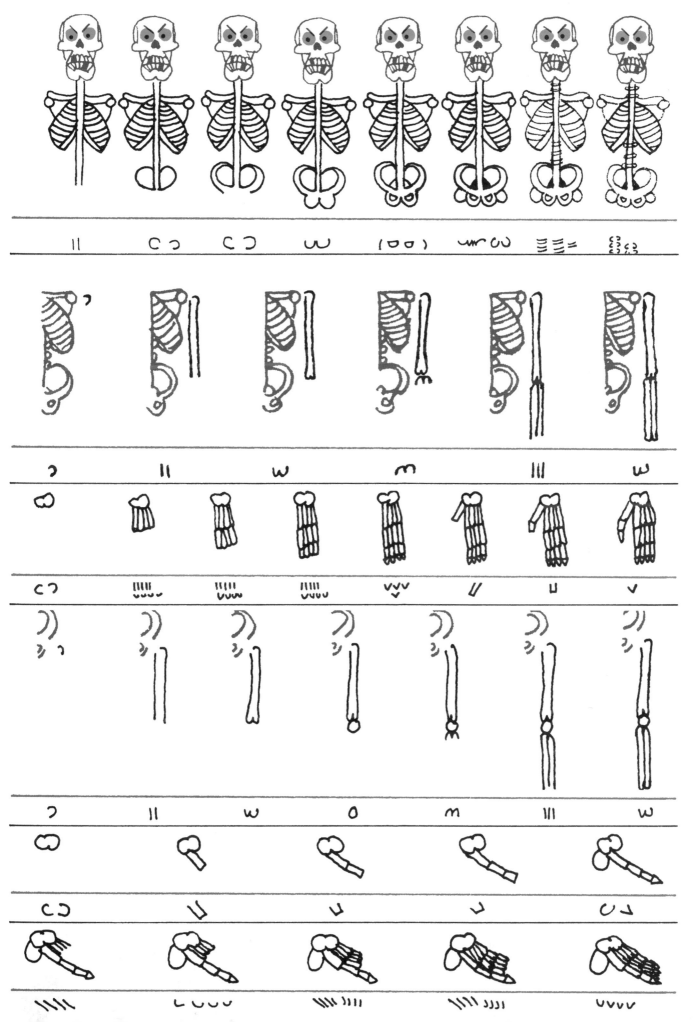

VAMPIRE

ALSO

23

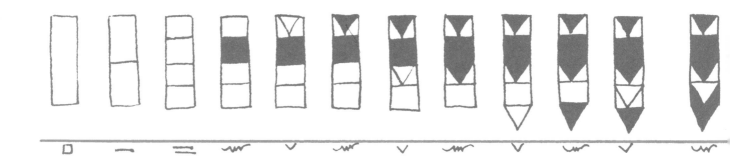

MR. HYDE

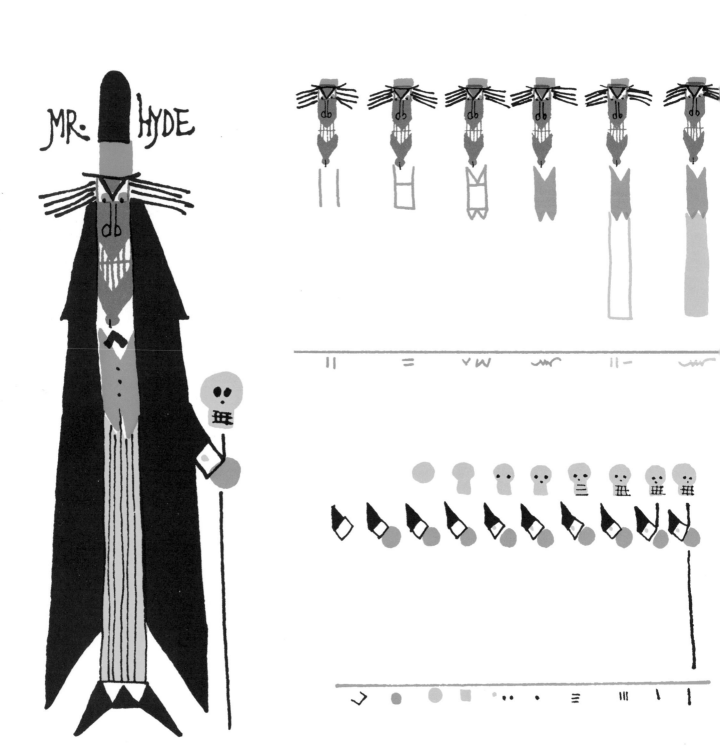

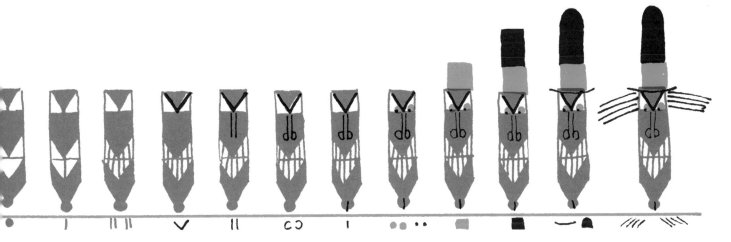

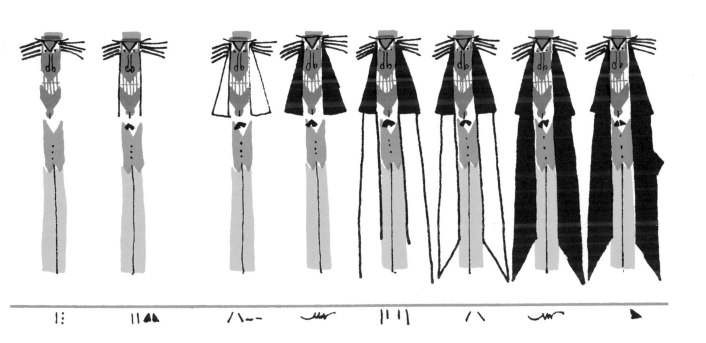

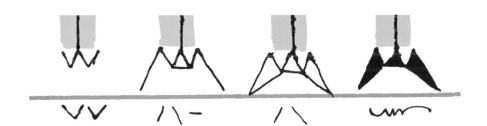

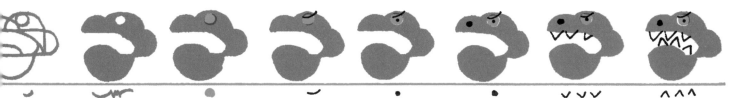

KING
CONGO

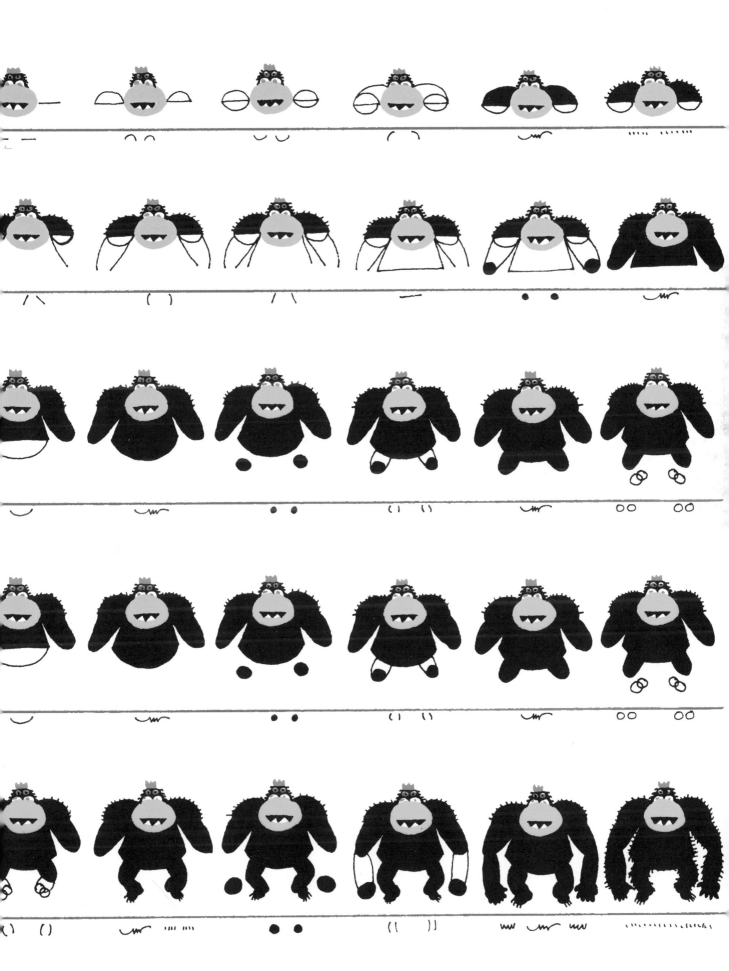

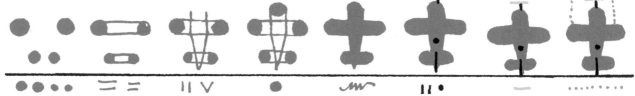

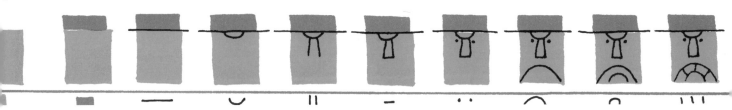

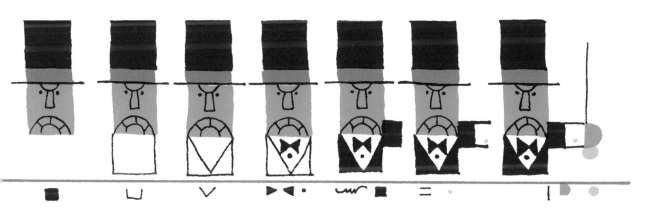

MR. HYDE

FOR MORE WEIRDOS, LOOK FOR:

Greengrin, Dr. Jekyll and Mr. Hyde,
Frank, Dracula, and Dracula's Car in
ED EMBERLEY'S
BIG GREEN DRAWING BOOK.

Kreegor the Neebort, Ogre,
Buttercup, and Vampirene in
ED EMBERLEY'S
BIG ORANGE DRAWING BOOK.

Swamp Creature in
ED EMBERLEY'S
BIG PURPLE DRAWING BOOK.

Bleezybub, Devil Dog,
Foodle, and Feedle in
ED EMBERLEY'S
BIG RED DRAWING BOOK.

Little, Brown Books for Young Readers

Hachette Book Group
237 Park Avenue, New York, NY 10017
Visit our Web site at www.lb-kids.com

LB kids is an imprint of Little, Brown Books for Young Readers.
The LB kids name and logo are trademarks of Hachette Book Group, Inc.

First Revised Paperback Edition: June 2005

ISBN 978-0-316-78971-4 (pb)
ISBN 978-0-316-23546-4 (hc)
LCCN 2001041744

PB: 10 9 8 7 6

WKT

Manufactured in China